INTRIGUING LATERAL THINKING PUZZLES

Paul Sloane & Des MacHale

Illustrated by
Myron Miller

Sterling Publishing Co., Inc.
New York

Acknowledgments

With acknowledgments and thanks to the Broughton family of Brecksville, Ohio, for The Sign, The Hasty Robber, The Hasty Packer, Untying the Ropes, The Painter, and Smart Appearance. Also to Mrs. Pat Woodfield of Camberley, England, for The Tree and the Axe.

• •

Edited by Claire Bazinet

Library of Congress Cataloging-in-Publication Data
Sloane, Paul, 1950–

    Intriguing lateral thinking puzzles/by Paul Sloane and Des MacHale; illustrated by Myron Miller.

    p.   cm.

    Includes index.

    ISBN 0-8069-4252-5

    1. Puzzles. I. MacHale, Des. II. Title.

    GV1493.S5937 1996

    793.73—dc20   95-53250

                                                CIP

10 9 8

Published by Sterling Publishing Company, Inc.
387 Park Avenue South, New York, N.Y. 10016
© 1996 by Paul Sloane and Des MacHale
Distributed in Canada by Sterling Publishing
℅ Canadian Manda Group, One Atlantic Avenue, Suite 105
Toronto, Ontario, Canada M6K 3E7
Distributed in Great Britain and Europe by Cassell PLC
Wellington House, 125 Strand, London WC2R 0BB, England
Distributed in Australia by Capricorn Link (Australia) Pty Ltd.
P.O. Box 6651, Baulkham Hills, Business Centre, NSW 2153, Australia
Manufactured in the United States of America
All rights reserved

Sterling ISBN 0-8069-4252-5

CONTENTS

INTRODUCTION

Lateral thinking puzzles are often strange situations which require an explanation. They are solved through a dialogue between the quizmaster, who sets the puzzle, and the solver or solvers, who try to figure out the answer. The puzzles, as presented, generally do not contain sufficient information for the solver to uncover the solution. So a key part of the process is the asking of questions. The questions can receive one of only three possible answers— yes, no, or irrelevant.

When one line of inquiry reaches an end, then another approach is needed, often from a completely new direction. This is where the lateral thinking comes in.

Some people find it frustrating that, for any puzzle, it is possible to construct various answers that fit the initial statement of the puzzle. However, for a good lateral thinking puzzle, the proper answer will be the "best"—in the sense of the most apt and satisfying. In real-life too, most problems have more than one possible solution. A good lateral thinker will not accept the first solution found but will continue to look for new and creative approaches.

The puzzles in this book range in difficulty from the Easy and Elementary up to the Fascinating and Fiendish. However, the first section, Dangerous and Deadly, is a collection of situations involving strange deaths or accidents. These were given their own section because many readers seem to like this kind of puzzle best. These problems teach you to check your assumptions about any situation. You need to be open-minded, flexible and creative in your questioning, and able to put lots of different clues and pieces of information together. Once you reach a viable solution you keep going in order to refine it or to replace it with a better solution. This is lateral thinking!

THE PUZZLES

Dangerous and Deadly Puzzles

The Deadly Melody

A woman heard a tune which she recognized. She took a gun and shot a stranger. Why?

Clues: 50/Answer: 78.

The Sign

A man and his wife were in their car. The man saw a sign. Without either of them saying a word, he drew a gun and shot his wife dead. Why?

Clues: 50/Answer: 86.

New Shoes

A woman bought a new pair of shoes and then went to work. She died. Why?

Clues: 50/Answer: 83.

The Archduke

When Archduke Ferdinand was shot, in 1914, his attendants could not undo his coat to stem his bleeding wound. Why not?

Clues: 50/Answer: 74.

The Hasty Packer

She died because she packed too quickly. How did she die?

Clues: 50–51/Answer: 80.

Heartless

A man who was surrounded by other people suddenly had a heart attack. Everyone saw this but no one intervened. He subsequently died. There was no ill-will towards him, and no physical barrier between him and the others. Why did no one try to help him?

Clue: 51/Answer: 80.

Dead Drunk

A man was coming home after a night out drinking. There was no one around, so he decided to relieve himself. Within minutes he was dead. What happened?

Clues: 51/Answer: 77–78.

The Big Room

A man is lying dead in a big room. Musical instruments lie around. He is holding a bottle of brandy. He died because of the brandy, but how?

Clues: 51/Answer: 74.

Sacrifice

Three castaways were starving on a desert island. When they had run out of food they decided that one of them had to die to be eaten by the other two. All three were single, of the same age, experience, size and skills. But they easily decided who should die. How?

Clues: 51/Answer: 86.

Stolen Finger

A man sneaked into a morgue one night and cut the little finger off a corpse. Why?

Clues: 51/Answer: 87.

Poor Dogs

During WWII, why did German soldiers have to shoot the dogs they had carefully trained?

Clues: 51/Answer: 84–85.

Radio Death

A man is driving his car. He turns on the radio and hears music. He stops and shoots himself. Why?

Clues: 52/Answer: 85.

Thirsty

A man dies of thirst in his own home. How come?

Clues: 52/Answer: 89.

After-Shave

A man is given a bottle of after-shave for his birthday. He puts some on and later that day he dies. How?

Clues: 52/Answer: 74.

Capsize

A riverboat in good condition is steaming down a calm river when it suddenly capsizes, drowning most of the passengers. What happened?

Clues: 52/Answer: 75.

Untying the Ropes

When they untied the ropes, everyone knew he was dead. How?

Clues: 52/Answer: 90–91.

Murder in the Newspaper

An old man read a report in his morning newspaper about a wealthy woman who had died of old age. "She was murdered!" he gasped. Then he carried on reading the rest of the newspaper. How did he know that it was murder and why did he do nothing about it?

Clues: 52/Answer: 83.

The Man Who Returned Too Soon

One bright sunny morning a man left his home. After some time he decided to return home and came back straightaway. When he got home he died. If he had not gone home so quickly he would have lived. What happened?

Clues: 53/Answer: 82.

The Truck Driver

A truck driver was driving along an empty highway when he sensed there was something wrong with his truck. He stopped and got out to look at it. He was then killed. How?

Clues: 53/Answer: 89–90.

The Perfect Murder

Edward carefully plotted the murder of his wife. One winter's day he strangled her in the bedroom, then faked a burglary. He ransacked the house, scattered possessions and broke through the patio doors. He set the burglar alarm downstairs before driving to the local golf course to establish his alibi. Two hours later, when Edward was in the middle of his golf game with three colleagues, the burglar alarm went off and the police were alerted. They found the house apparently broken into and the wife strangled. No animals or electrical devices were found which could have set the alarm off, so it looked as though an intruder had set off the alarm before killing the poor woman. Edward was never arrested or charged. The police inspector long suspected Edward, but there was one question which he could not fathom: How did the suspect get the burglar alarm to go off so conveniently? Can you work it out?

Clues: 53–54/Answer: 84.

The Circle and the Line

They died because the circle crossed the line. Explain.

Clues: 54/Answer: 76.

The Sniper

A man is driving in a war zone when he is attacked by a sniper. His car skids and turns over. He manages to crawl out and get behind his car but he is still under fire from the sniper. He has no gun. All he has is a bottle of water, a handkerchief, and a cigarette lighter. How does he escape?

Clues: 54/Answer: 86.

Fair Deal

Several truck drivers at a roadside café started to play poker. The pot was large and the game was serious. Suddenly one of the men accused the dealer of cheating. The dealer drew a knife and, in plain view of all the others, stabbed the man and killed him. The police were called and they interviewed everyone who had been present. But no man was arrested or charged with any offense. Why not?

Clues: 54/Answer: 79.

The Cloth

A man waved a cloth and another man died. Why?

Clues: 54/Answer: 76–77.

Easy and Elementary Puzzles

Bostonian

....

A man was born in Boston, Massachusetts. Both his parents were born in Boston, Massachusetts. He lived all his life in Boston but he was not a United States citizen. How come?

Clues: 55/Answer: 74–75.

The Tree and the Axe

....

A woman bought a young tree and put it in her garden. The next day she took an axe to it. Why?

Clues: 55/Answer: 89.

Below Par

A middle-aged man took up golf for the first time and within a month he went around his local course in under 90 shots. However, he was not pleased. Why?

Clue: 55/Answer: 74.

School Friend

Joe went back to his hometown and met an old school friend he had not seen for years. His friend said, "I am married now but not to anyone you know. This is my daughter."

Joe turned to the little girl and asked her her name. She said, "I have the same name as my mother."

"Then you must be called Louise," said Joe. He was right, but how did he know?

Clues: 55/Answer: 86.

Sell More Beer

A management consultant went into a bar one evening. After a little while he told the bar owner a simple and quite legal way of selling a lot more beer. However, the bar owner was not pleased. Why not?

Clues: 55/Answer: 86.

The Lumberjacks

Tim and Joe are two lumberjacks who work at the same rate of speed. One morning, Tim works steadily from 8 o'clock to noon without taking a break. Joe starts and finishes at the same times, but he takes a five-minute break every half-hour. At the end of the period Joe has felled considerably more trees than Tim. How come?

Clue: 56/Answer: 82.

The Clinch

A prim lady was disgusted that the teenage boy and girl in front of her at the cinema remained locked in a passionate embrace throughout the entire feature. She called the manager, who immediately summoned an ambulance. Why?

Clue: 56/Answer: 76.

Precognition

A lady knocked at the door of a tiny cottage and when an old lady opened the door she said, "Good morning, Mrs. Turner." Neither of them had ever met, or seen or heard of the other before. How did she know the old lady's name?

Clue: 56/Answer: 85.

Dud Car

The Chevrolet Nova was a successful car in many countries but not in Mexico. Why not?

Clues: 56/Answer: 79.

Red Light

A police officer was sitting on his motorcycle at a red traffic light when two teenagers in a sports car drove by him at 50 miles per hour. He did not chase them or try to apprehend them. Why not?

Clues: 56/Answer: 85-86.

Nun-plussed

A priest sitting in a doctor's waiting room was horrified to see a crying nun, rushing from the doctor's surgery, followed by a flustered doctor. Angrily he asked the doctor for an explanation. What explanation did the doctor give?

Clue: 56/Answer: 83.

Confectionery Manufacturer

A manufacturer of confectionery has a work force of thousands of workers. They never strike or demand better conditions. They work up to twenty hours per day and receive no wages except food and shelter. Yet every year a completely new work force is brought in and none of the existing workers is re-employed. Why?

Clues: 56/Answer: 77.

The Painter

Much of his painting was seen at the city's two large art galleries but no one had ever heard of him. Why not?

Clues: 57/Answer: 84.

Regular Arguments

Every evening a man and a woman would eat at a table and then have a violent argument, swearing, shouting and insulting each other. The rest of the time they got on very well, with never a cross word. Why did they argue every night?

Clues: 57/Answer: 86.

Beautiful Girls

As a group of sailors emerged from their ship after months at sea, one spindly wimp bet his fellow sailors that he would have a beautiful girl on each arm within an hour. How did he win his bet?

Clue: 57/Answer: 74.

Orange Trick

There is an orange in the middle of a circular table. Without touching or moving the orange or the table how could you place a second orange under the first?

Clue: 57/Answer: 84.

The Fall

A man fell 140 feet (43m) without a parachute. He turned upside down seven times and came to land safely on solid ground. How come?

Clues: 57/Answer: 79.

The Bookmark

A man who needs a bookmark is offered a fine bookmark for a dollar. Why does he refuse it?

Clue: 57/Answer: 74.

Good-bye, Mother

A young woman in a restaurant was approached by a tearful old lady who said, "You look so like my own daughter who passed away last year. Could you do me a favor and say 'Good-bye, Mother' when I leave?"

The young woman happily agreed and said, "Good-bye, Mother" when the old lady left. Later she got a shock. What was it?

Clue: 57/Answer: 80.

Steer Clear of the Banks

A man drove into town and parked at the end of the main street. He got out of his car and went up to the bookstore at the opposite end of the street. He then came back down the street to his car and drove off. There are three banks on the main street, but the man did not walk past any of them. Why not?

Clue: 58/Answer: 87.

A Hairy Story

A man who was completely bald met a doctor at a party. She had lovely short black hair. He explained that he had tried hair restorers and transplants but without any success. She sympathized. "If you could make my hair look like yours, I would gladly pay you $1000," he said.

"O.K., I'll do it," she answered. How did she win the $1000?

Clues: 58/Answer: 80.

By the River

A police officer saw a man standing by a river holding a loaded gun near his head. The officer rushed towards the man and grabbed the gun. A minute later he handed the gun back with apologies. Why?

Clues: 58/Answer: 75.

WALLY Test

Sharpen your pencil and your wits! Here comes a WALLY Test. Write out your answers to these quickfire questions:

1. In Camberley, England, two out of every seven people have telephone numbers that are not listed in the directory. If there are 14,000 names in the Camberley telephone directory, how many of them have numbers that are unlisted?

2. In Iran, a Westerner cannot take a photograph of a man with a turban. Why not?

3. How many successful parachute jumps does a trainee parachutist in the U.S. Army have to make before he graduates from jump school?

4. What is the invention, first discovered in ancient times, that allows people to see through solid walls?

5. A man carefully pointed his car due east and then drove for two miles. He was then two miles west of where he started from. How come?

6. A mail plane was halfway from Dallas to Miami at a height of 2000 feet on a clear, still day. It dropped a 100 kg sack of airmail letters and a 100 kg steel rod at the same time. Which hit the ground first?

7. If two are company and three are a crowd, what are four and five?

8. With which hand does a nun stir her coffee?

9. Why do some people press elevator buttons with their fingers and others with their thumbs?

10. What do you say to a man who claims not to be superstitious?

11. If a grandfather clock strikes thirteen, what time is it?

12. Two sons, two fathers and a grandfather sat together. How many men were there?

13. An archaeologist showed his daughter a coin that he had found on a dig. He told her it was dated 200 B.C. She told him she thought it was a fake. Who was right?

14. For this two-parter, tell us: a) What color is a refrigerator? b) What do cows drink?

See WALLY answers on page 92.

• •

Intriguing and Interesting Puzzles

The Helicopter

A helicopter was hovering 200 feet above the sea when the pilot suddenly turned off the engine. The rotor stopped but the helicopter did not crash. Why not?

Clues: 59/Answer: 81.

Car in the River

A man was driving alone in his car when he spun off the road at high speed. He crashed through a fence and bounced down a steep ravine before the car plunged into a fast-flowing river. As the car slowly settled in the river, the man realized that his arm was broken and that he could not release his seat belt and get out of the car. The car sank to the bottom of the river. He was trapped in the car. Rescuers arrived two hours later, yet they found him alive. How come?

Clues: 59/Answer: 75.

Call Box

A lady depended on a public telephone call box to make calls but it was frequently out of order. Each day she reported the problem to the telephone company but nothing was done. Finally she phoned the company with a false piece of information which caused the telephone to be fixed within hours. What did she tell them?

Clues: 59/Answer: 75.

The Typist

A young woman applied for a job as a secretary and typist. There were dozens of applicants. The woman could type only eleven words per minute, yet she got the job. Why?

Clues: 59/Answer: 90.

Two Jugs

A man had a jug full of lemonade and a jug full of milk. He poured them both into one large vat, yet he kept the lemonade separate from the milk. How?

Clues: 59–60/Answer: 90.

Speeding Ticket

A man is driving his car at ten miles an hour down a quiet suburban street when a police officer spots him and fines him for speeding. Why?

Clues: 60/Answer: 87

Twin Trouble

Bob and Sam were identical twins born in London in 1911. Bob was born before Sam but Sam was older than Bob. How come?

Clues: 60/Answer: 90.

Library Lunacy

A public library suddenly announced that each member could borrow up to ten books and not return them for up to six months. Why?

Clues: 60/Answer: 82.

Elevator

A woman was in an elevator. She was frightened. She sat down. She laughed and stood up. Why?

Clues: 60/Answer: 79

Fall of the Wall

In its day, the Great Wall of China was considered virtually impregnable, yet it was breached within a few years of being built. How?

Clues: 60/Answer: 79.

Smart Appearance

Victor was smartly dressed, well shaven, and with the best haircut he had had for years. Many of his friends and relatives saw him, yet no one complimented him. Why not?

Clues: 61/Answer: 86.

Dogs Home

A boy brings home a lost puppy but his parents order him to dispose of it. As he walks into town, wondering what to do, he sees a truck with DOGS HOME printed on it. He slips the puppy into the truck, but this leads to a minor disaster. Why?

Clues: 61/Answer: 78

Title Role

A vain actress was thrilled to hear from her agent that she had received the title role in the movie of a famous book. But later she was very displeased. Why?

Clues: 61/Answer: 89.

Job Lot

A builder was very pleased to buy a job lot of bricks at a very low price. When he examined them he found that they were sound, strong and well made, but he was extremely unhappy. Why?

Clues: 61/Answer: 81.

The Lifeboat

A man was cast adrift in a lifeboat. He was horrified to see that it was letting in water, so he diligently bailed out the water. After two days, he did not bother bailing out the water anymore. Why not?

Clues: 61/Answer: 82.

Invaluable

A man got something of little value. It became very valuable so he threw it away. If it had been worth less, he would have kept it. Why?

Clues: 61/Answer: 81.

The Crash

In heavy fog, there was a serious road crash which involved two trucks and six cars. All the vehicles were severely damaged. Police and ambulances were quickly on the scene, where they found both truck drivers and took them to the hospital for treatment. However, no drivers from any of the cars could be found at the scene of the accident. Why not?

Clues: 62/Answer: 77.

Westward Ho!

(West) Bristol ———— Reading ———— London (East)

Two men set off on foot one morning. They started from Reading and headed east towards London. They walked until they reached a restaurant where they sat down and had lunch. They then carried on walking east towards London. They arrived that same afternoon in Bristol. Since the only direction in which they walked was east, how was it possible for them to arrive in Bristol?

Clues: 62/Answer: 91.

40 Feet Ahead

A man set out for a walk. At the end of his walk his head had travelled 40 feet farther than his feet had travelled. He was a healthy man with all his limbs intact before and after the walk. So how did his head travel farther than his feet?

Clues: 62/Answer: 79–80.

The Circular Table

A lady has an expensive circular oak table and she wishes to find its exact center. How does she do this without marking the table in any way?

Clues: 63/Answer: 76.

T-Shirts

A change in the law in Italy resulted in large sales of white T-shirts with black bands on them. How come?

Clues: 63/Answer: 88.

Two Suitcases

A man is carrying two suitcases, one in each hand. One is a big empty suitcase. The other is a smaller light suitcase full of books. He puts the smaller suitcase into the bigger one, making it heavy and difficult to carry. Why does he do this?

Clues: 63/Answer: 90.

The Nonchalant Police Officer

One fine morning, a police officer was walking down the high street in the middle of town. Turning a corner, he gasped as he saw two armed robbers dash out of a bank, firing guns as they left. He then ignored them, and continued on walking up the street. Why?

Clues: 63/Answer: 83.

Challenging and Chastening Puzzles

Rare Event

What happened in the second half of the 20th century and will not happen again for over 4000 years?

Clues: 64/Answer: 85.

Holy Orders

A priest goes into a church carrying a loaded gun. Why? (P.S. He was not a canon!)

Clues: 64/Answer: 81.

Well Dressed

Why did an old lady always answer the door wearing her hat and coat?

Clues: 64/Answer: 91.

Kid Stuff

Many more children are involved as pedestrians in road accidents than might be expected from their numbers and road use. An expert on road accidents has put forward an ingenious theory to account for this. What do you think the theory might be?

Clues: 64/Answer: 82.

The Two Drivers

Two drivers drove slowly and safely in the correct direction down a wide road before coming to a stop in front of a red stop light. A nearby police officer immediately arrested one of the drivers and let the other one drive off. The police officer had never seen or heard of either driver before. Neither driver had a criminal record. They were both fully dressed and no one had been drinking. Both cars were in excellent roadworthy condition and had not been stolen. The arrested driver was charged and convicted. Of what?

Clues: 65/Answer: 90.

Keys in the Car

A man locks his keys inside his car and is unable to get them out despite trying for an hour. A police officer comes along and offers to help. He discovers that the back door of the car is unlocked and he consequently recovers the keys. The man thanks him, but when the officer departs the man locks the back door, leaving the keys inside. Why?

Clues: 65/Answer: 81.

The Hasty Robber

A man robbed a bank. If he had seen the other gun he would not have been in such a hurry. Why not?

Clues: 65/Answer: 80.

How to Choose a Builder

A man wanted to construct an important building and he received tenders from a hundred builders, who each presented their qualifications and claimed to be the best builder around. How did he eventually choose between them?

Clues: 66/Answer: 81.

The Unlucky Gambler

A very unlucky gambler had lost all his money. His friends organized a raffle, rigged so that he would be sure to win. Knowing the ticket number he held, they filled a hat with tickets bearing the same number. They then had him draw the winning number. "Well," they asked him, "who won?"

"Not me, anyway," he replied sadly. What had happened?

Clue: 66/Answer: 90.

Brush-off

Amanda was doing something important when she received a phone call from Zoe, who was long-winded and boring. How did Amanda quickly finish the call without offending Zoe?

Clues: 66/Answer: 75.

The Code

The doorman at an exclusive club says one word to each prospective entrant. If the entrant answers correctly he is allowed to enter; otherwise, he is rejected.

A hopeful non-member observed carefully as a member approached. The doorman said, "Twelve." The member replied, "Six." He was admitted. A second member came up. The doorman said, "Six." The member replied, "Three." He was admitted. The man now decided that this was easy and he stepped forward. The doorman said, "Ten." The man replied, "Five." The doorman angrily kicked him out. What should he have said?

Clues: 66/Answer: 77.

Time of Arrival

A teenage boy returned home from a party very late and silently crept upstairs to his bedroom. No one saw or heard him arrive. Next morning when his mother asked him what time he had arrived home, he replied, "About one o'clock." How did she know that he had, in fact, arrived much later?

Clues: 66–67/Answer: 89.

Depressurization

A pilot was flying alone at 30,000 feet altitude when he heard a rattling noise in the plane. He immediately depressurized the plane, i.e., let the air out and allowed the pressure in the plane to drop to that of the outside atmosphere. A sudden depressurization is generally considered very dangerous, so why did he do this?

Clues: 67/Answer: 78.

A Solution of Paint

A problem which had caused the loss of many thousands of lives and the loss of millions of dollars worth of property was solved with a can of paint and a brush. What was the problem?

Clue: 67/Answer: 87.

Strange Reactions

John and Joan, who both enjoyed their work, were given surprises one morning. John was told that he was being laid off that week because there was no further work for him. Joan was told that she was being promoted and would get a pay raise. Joan cried for the rest of the day, while John laughed. Why?

Clues: 67/Answer: 87.

Striking the Elephant

A man uses a stick to strike a part of an elephant and after a few seconds it disappears. The man is then a lot richer. Why?

Clues: 67/Answer: 87.

The Archaeologist

A professor of archaeology was on an excavation at a site when he found an ancient and interesting item. He took it home and put it in his study. His wife and children were away so there was no other person in the house. He locked up and went to bed. In the morning, he was horrified to find the item gone. A thorough search showed it was not in the house. There had been no break-in and no one else had entered or left the house. What had happened?

Clues: 67/Answer: 74.

The Deadly Diamonds

A Bedouin prince had three diamonds which he kept in a box with a sliding lid that he kept firmly closed. The box also contained two deadly cobras which would attack any stranger foolish enough to open the box. One day a thief sneaked into the prince's tent and within moments had safely stolen the diamonds. How did he do it?

Clues: 67–68/Answer: 78.

Gaze Away

A man walked into a room full of normal people. None of them would look him in the eye. Why not?

Clues: 68/Answer: 80.

Desert

A man walked alone for days across a desert. He did not take water or any kind of drink with him. He did not find water. How did he survive?

Clues: 68/Answer: 78.

The Container

King Arthur gave one of the knights of the Round Table a bottomless metal container in which for many years he kept flesh and blood. What was it?

Clue: 68/Answer: 77.

Mutilation

Why did a man deliberately douse himself with sulfuric acid?

Clues: 68/Answer: 83.

Fascinating and Fiendish Puzzles

Cowardly Act
....

Why did a coward deliberately expose himself to significant danger?

Clues: 69/Answer: 77.

Fall of the Hall
....

A well-designed and structurally sound building owned by the government suddenly collapsed. Why did this happen?

Clues: 69/Answer: 79.

The Cicada
....

There is one kind of cicada (an insect sometimes known as a cricket) which has a 17-year life cycle. It lives dormant, underground, for 16 years as a grub, then emerges for one year as an active insect. What possible survival advantage can such a 17-year life cycle have?

Clue: 69/Answer: 76.

Sweet in Pocket

· ·

Because he had a sweet in his pocket, a man invented something which is found in most modern kitchens. What is it?

Clues: 69/Answer: 88.

Stringing Along

· ·

A man carefully glued tiny pieces of glass to a length of string. At first he was very pleased with the results. But later he regretted doing it. Why?

Clues: 69–70/Answer: 87–88.

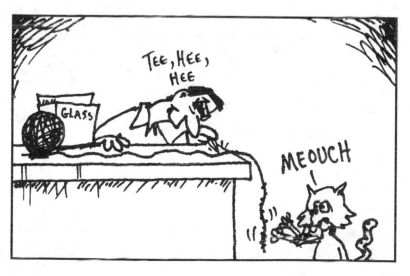

The Painting

A painter gave his aunt an ugly abstract painting which she stored in the attic. However, when he came to stay she hurriedly hung it on the wall of her parlor, but unfortunately she hung it upside down. What did she say when he pointed this out?

Clues: 70/Answer: 84.

Mickey Mouse's Girlfriend

Why were a group of grown men running around asking each other who was Mickey Mouse's girlfriend?

Clues: 70/Answer: 82.

The Parcel

Why did a lady deliberately leave a parcel behind her on a bus?

Clues: 70/Answer: 84.

The Suitcase and the Box

A man came out of a large building carrying a suitcase and box. He was very happy. He went into a smaller building and a few minutes later emerged from the smaller building very angry and carrying just the suitcase. What was going on?

Clues: 70/Answer: 88.

Third Place

A man enters a competition confidently expecting to win, but he only comes in third. However, he is very amused. Why?

Clues: 70/Answer: 89.

The Missing Diamond

A man kept a precious diamond in a safe. Nobody else knew the combination. It was not written down. Nobody ever saw him open the safe. Yet one day when he opened the safe, the diamond was gone. How come?

Clues: 71/Answer: 82–83.

Paddle Your Own Canoe

A man set out to paddle his canoe down a slowly flowing river from one point to another. He found that no matter how quickly he paddled, it made no difference to the time it took for his journey. Why not?

Clues: 71/Answer: 84.

Poor Impersonation

An actress is hired to impersonate an heiress who has died. The actress looks very much like the heiress. Her acting is superb. She watches videos of the woman and works tirelessly in front of a mirror to develop an excellent imitation of the woman's appearance, mannerisms and voice. Yet she is soon exposed as an impostor. Why?

Clues: 71/Answer: 85.

Doctor's Appointment

A woman has an appointment to visit the doctor. When she gets there the receptionist tells her that there is a new doctor and that he cannot see the woman just yet as he is on the telephone. The woman waits and then the doctor calls her in and says that he is sorry he kept her waiting but he had some important telephone calls to handle. Within moments the doctor is highly embarrassed. Why?

Clues: 71/Answer: 78.

Creepy Crawlies

A man moves into a new house and finds that his garden is crawling with insects, slugs, snails, caterpillars and unwanted bugs. He goes to his local cinema, community hall and bars (where he knows nobody) and asks for a donation to help clear his garden. Everyone responds very generously and he is able to solve his problem. What happened?

Clues: 71/Answer: 77.

Sweet Wheat

A farmer wins first prize for his wheat every year in an agricultural show in stiff competition with his neighboring farmers. However, after the show is over, he sends each of his fellow competitors a bag of his best wheat seed. Why?

Clues: 72/Answer: 88.

Three Notes

One morning a woman wrote the same note to three different people. The first was a bank robber, who laughed at the note and threw it away. The second was a Bolivian, who also threw the note away. The third was a priest, who was very sad to receive the note. What was happening?

Clues: 72/Answer: 89.

Catching a Bullet

A man fires a bullet from a gun and another man catches the bullet with his bare hands. The bullet does not touch anything (except air, of course) from the gun to the hand. The second man is uninjured. How does he do it? (There are two good solutions to this problem. Can you find them both?)

Clues: 72/Answers: 75–76.

THE CLUES

Dangerous and Deadly Puzzles

The Deadly Melody

She was in her home when this happened.

She had heard the tune many times before. Normally she was happy when she heard this tune.

The stranger was trying to rob her.

The Sign

The sign was inside the car and the car was stationary.

He shot her because he learned she had been having an affair.

New Shoes

She died because she wore the new shoes.

She was involved in entertainment.

The Archduke

He was very vain.

His coat had no buttons or zippers.

The Hasty Packer

She packed one essential item for a particular kind of journey.

She packed material and string.

Heartless

The man's profession is important.

Dead Drunk

He died an accidental death as a result of his actions and where he was.

He was alone at a subway station.

The Big Room

He died because he went back for the brandy.

He drowned.

Sacrifice

They did not choose by chance but agreed between them based on a good reason, which even the one chosen had to admit was sound.

They had different beliefs and philosophies.

Stolen Finger

He wanted to send it to someone.

He wanted someone to think it was his finger.

Poor Dogs

They had trained the dogs with the intention of inflicting harm on enemies.

The dogs did exactly what they had been trained to do.

Radio Death

He had been expecting to hear the piece of music that he heard, but had not planned to commit suicide.

There was something about the way the music was playing which meant that he was in very serious trouble.

Thirsty

The man was fit and not hampered in his movements.

There was plenty of water in and near his home.

After-Shave

He died an accidental death.

He died because his smell was different.

Capsize

It overbalanced when the weight distribution on the boat suddenly changed.

Something quite light dropped onto one side of the boat.

Untying the Ropes

Ropes were not involved in the way the man died, nor was he tied up in the ropes.

Untying the ropes was a form of signal.

Murder in the Newspaper

His profession is important.

He had met the murderer.

The Man Who Returned Too Soon

He died an accidental death. No other person or creature was involved.

The danger was not in his home. What killed him was the fact that he returned too quickly.

The Truck Driver

He was killed accidentally. No other person or creature was involved.

He had sensed that something was wrong with his truck. He was right. His death and the problem with the truck were linked.

The Perfect Murder

He had caused something to fall so that its motion would be detected by the burglar alarm sensors.

No electrical, telephone, or radio devices were used. He

did not use any spring or complex mechanical device. He used something much simpler.

The Circle and the Line

They died an accidental death in the course of a journey.

They could see the line drawing nearer. However, the line never moved.

The Sniper

The sniper is determined to shoot him and will come to the car to do so if he takes cover.

Attack is the best form of defense.

Fair Deal

There was nothing faked or pretended about this incident. The dealer had murdered the man who was stabbed.

The dealer was punished for the crime.

The Cloth

The man who waved the cloth knew that his action would probably cause a man to die.

He did not know which man would die.

The man died of a gunshot.

Easy and Elementary Puzzles

Bostonian

There was nothing strange or unusual about this man.

His friends and neighbors in Boston were also not U.S. citizens.

The Tree and the Axe

She used the axe to destroy the tree that she had recently bought.

She did not buy the tree in order to put it into the garden.

Below Par

He was not pleased because it was not a good score.

School Friend

Joe did not know who had married his friend. He had no other source of information than this conversation.

He knew that the girl's mother was called Louise.

Sell More Beer

The consultant gave the bar owner a piece of advice that many of the bar's customers would have been glad to hear.

Implementing the advice would benefit the customers more than the bar owner.

The Lumberjacks

During his breaks, Joe does something which helps him to cut more trees.

The Clinch

Something caused them to be locked together even though they wanted to part.

Precognition

The profession of the lady who knocked at the door is important.

Dud Car

The Nova had a poor image, even though it was a good automobile.

People laughed when they heard of it.

Red Light

The police officer was perfectly capable of chasing the teenagers and he was not engaged in any other task at the time.

The officer was conscientious and always chased and apprehended those he saw breaking the law.

Nun-plussed

The doctor smiled and explained that he had cured the nun's complaint.

Confectionery Manufacturer

The confectionery is a popular and healthy food.

The workers are always very busy.

The Painter

He was a very good painter whose work could be seen at art galleries and private houses.

He was not shy of publicity and he used his own name.

He did not paint on canvas.

Regular Arguments

It was the same topic and conversation which led them to quarrel every night.

On Saturdays they argued in the afternoon as well.

Beautiful Girls

He paid in order to get a beautiful girl on each arm.

Orange Trick

The second orange goes under the first orange but the first orange remains on the table.

The Fall

The man had no special skills or training. Many other people can do this.

Some people find this kind of fall enjoyable. Others are terrified.

The Bookmark

He has what he considers a better alternative.

Good-bye, Mother

The old lady had a mean purpose in mind when she asked the young woman the favor.

Steer Clear of the Banks

Roller-blading, cycling and running were all forbidden on the road.

A Hairy Story

No wigs, potions or transplants were involved.

After her actions, his hair looked exactly like hers.

By the River

The man had intended to fire the gun.

No one was in danger.

He would not have used the gun if he had not been near the river.

Intriguing and Interesting Puzzles

The Helicopter

It was a real helicopter hovering over a real sea. The helicopter stopped flying and stopped hovering, but it did not hit the sea.

The helicopter was owned by an oil company.

Car in the River

He did not have any special equipment or powers.

He breathed normally throughout the whole incident.

Call Box

She gave the telephone company a strong incentive to fix the call box.

She told the telephone company that some people were very pleased that the telephone did not work properly.

The Typist

She was chosen on merit.

She was a good typist.

Two Jugs

There was no divider in the vat; it was one large container.

After the pourings, the vat contained all the lemonade and all the milk—yet they were separate.

If you could have heard the operation, you would know the answer.

Speeding Ticket

It was not a one-way street and there was nothing wrong or unusual about the car.

He was breaking the general speed limit.

Twin Trouble

They were normal natural twins.

Bob was born first. The birth certificate correctly showed Sam's time of birth as before Bob's.

Library Lunacy

The library benefited from this temporary change in the rules.

This relaxation of the normal rules of borrowing was a one-time event caused by something else which was happening at the library.

Elevator

She was not alone in the elevator.

There was a misunderstanding.

Fall of the Wall

The construction of the wall was sound. It did not have any structural or mechanical weaknesses.

The wall was breached through subtlety rather than through force.

Smart Appearance

Professional help had been involved in making Victor look particularly smart.

Everyone noticed how smart he looked but no one spoke to him.

Dogs Home

The truck had two doors at the back.

One door was open and one was closed.

Title Role

She had been given the role of a beautiful and successful woman.

The book is by Daphne du Maurier. It concerns a woman who dies under mysterious circumstances.

Job Lot

They had been designed for a specific purpose.

They would be very useful for one type of building.

The Lifeboat

He was not rescued during the two days, nor did he see land or any other refuge.

The lifeboat was old-fashioned in design and construction.

Invaluable

The man was a criminal.

He was both lucky and unlucky.

The Crash

The police were not surprised that they could not find any drivers for the cars.

No one had left the scene of the accident.

Westward Ho!

They walked only in an eastward direction. They never reached or passed through London.

The location of the restaurant is important.

40 Feet Ahead

He was a normal man who walked in a normal fashion.

It was a long walk.

The Circular Table

She solved the problem easily and without special equipment.

She used a piece of paper.

T-Shirts

The T-shirts were designed to circumvent the law.

The law was a traffic regulation.

The black band was a diagonal stripe.

Two Suitcases

He does not intend to carry the suitcase far.

He is trying to save money.

The Nonchalant Police Officer

He was not cowardly or neglecting his duty.

No one else in the street took any notice of the robbers, even though they were seen by several passers-by.

Challenging and Chastening Puzzles

Rare Event

This is not an astronomical, geological or physical event.

The answer relates to the date. It last happened in the days of the Beatles and John F. Kennedy.

Holy Orders

The priest was a real priest carrying a real gun. He was not a criminal and no crime was involved.

He wanted to shoot something.

The gun was used to solve an unsightly problem.

Well Dressed

She was not cold and did not need to wear her hat and coat.

She did it for her convenience and to avoid a difficult situation.

She liked to chat but only to her friends.

Kid Stuff

The expert's theory has nothing to do with the behavior of children.

It has to do with the appearance of children to the motorist.

The Two Drivers

Although the two drivers had driven in identical fashion, one had committed an offense and the other had not. The police officer acted properly.

It happened in a hot country.

Keys in the Car

The man did not mean to lock his keys in the car. He had no criminal or ulterior motive. It was an accident.

When he had been unable to retrieve his keys, the man had initiated another course of action in order to get them.

The Hasty Robber

The other gun was not in the bank.

He was apprehended by the police. But not for robbery.

How to Choose a Builder

He had no knowledge of building or of the builders' experience.

He did not decide on price. He wanted a reliable builder of good reputation and quality.

He enlisted the help of the builders in selecting one who met his requirements.

The Unlucky Gambler

He had drawn a ticket from the hat but it did not bear the number 77. The only things that his friends had put in the hat were tickets with the number 77.

Brush-off

Amanda did not invent any excuse or pretense.

She wanted Zoe to think that they had been accidentally interrupted.

The Code

The members and the doorman were consistent and logical in what they said and did. There was a code based solely on the numbers, which they followed.

The code would work in other languages but probably with different combinations of numbers. (For example, in Italian the doorman might say "Otto" and the member reply, "Quattro."

Time of Arrival

The mother deduced correctly from what she saw that he must have arrived in very late.

When he came in, the boy did not make a sound. He removed his boots and then crept up to bed.

Depressurization

He did this for his own safety.

The rattle alerted him to a problem which might become dangerous.

A Solution of Paint

The problem concerned transportation. The use of the paint stopped overloading.

Strange Reactions

Joan was pleased at the news of her promotion. John was disappointed to learn that he was losing his job.

The nature of their work is important.

Striking the Elephant

The man is very skillful in his use of the stick.

The man strikes something made of ivory.

The Archaeologist

The item had been removed from the house.

When his wife was away, the archaeologist went for a walk every morning and evening. When she was at home, they took turns going for walks.

The Deadly Diamonds

The thief did not use any special powers or materials to subdue or control the snakes.

The thief opened the box in a way which allowed him to safely extract the diamonds.

Gaze Away

The man was physically normal, yet he was different from all the other people.

Everyone treated him with great respect.

Desert

People need to have water in their bodies in order to survive. How did the man get it?

No other person or creature is involved.

He did not find liquids of any kind in the desert.

The Container

It was a common article then and now.

Mutilation

The man was a criminal.

He hoped to escape detection.

Fascinating and Fiendish Puzzles

Cowardly Act

He risked pain and physical injury because he thought that he might thereby avoid a greater risk.

He hoped to get shot.

Fall of the Hall

No animal activity or change in the state of the building components or structure is involved.

It had been used for a different purpose than that for which it was designed.

The Cicada

It is thought that the 17-year life cycle of the cicada gives it additional protection against predators. But it is not safer underground than any other such grub, nor safer as an insect than any other cicada.

Sweet in Pocket

The man noticed that the sweet in his pocket was affected by something with which he was experimenting.

The invention is used in cooking.

Stringing Along

He used the string in a competition.

He gained an unfair advantage over his rivals.

The Painting

She tried not to hurt his feelings.

She claimed to like and understand the painting.

Mickey Mouse's Girlfriend

It was a deadly serious exercise.

It was a test.

The Parcel

It was something that she made for someone else.

She knew it would probably be found and handed in.

The Suitcase and the Box

He had gained his freedom but lost something dear to him.

The suitcase and the box had contained the personal belongings he had had for several years.

The smaller building was a bar into which he had gone to celebrate and to show off the contents of the box.

Third Place

It was an acting contest.

The man was a famous actor and movie star.

The contest was for fun.

The Missing Diamond

An enterprising thief had worked out a way of figuring out the combination.

The thief had left something in the room.

Paddle Your Own Canoe

The man and the canoe were normal, but the river was unusual.

He could do this only at a certain time of year.

Poor Impersonation

The actress was found out because she had used a mirror to rehearse.

Her voice was faultless. She looked exactly like the heiress in all regards except one.

Doctor's Appointment

The doctor and the woman had never met and there was no prior connection between them.

The doctor was embarrassed when he found out why the woman was there.

The doctor was trying to create a good impression on his first day.

Creepy Crawlies

He poisoned the bugs.

The places he went gave him what was worthless to them but useful to him.

Sweet Wheat

His primary concern is to ensure that his wheat will be of the finest quality.

He is quite happy for his neighbors to grow his strain of wheat and thereby produce better wheat. He gains by this.

Three Notes

She had never met any of the three people and had no intention of meeting them, but her note was a serious communication.

The bank robber was part of a gang and had a specific role in the planned robbery.

The Bolivian was a tourist.

Catching a Bullet

The second man had no special powers or protection. However, in each solution he would need very precise positioning.

The bullet is a normal bullet fired from a normal gun and is normally deadly.

When the man catches the bullet, it is travelling slowly.

THE ANSWERS

After-Shave

The man was a bee-keeper. The after-shave changed his smell and the swarm of bees that knew him well now attacked him as a stranger.

The Archaeologist

The ancient item was a dinosaur bone. When the professor's dog found the bone he took it out through the cat-flap and buried it in the garden!

The Archduke

Archduke Ferdinand's uniform was sewn onto him so that he looked immaculately smart. It could not be removed quickly. His desire for a perfect appearance probably cost him his life.

Beautiful Girls

He had the two beautiful girls tattooed on his arms.

Below Par

It was a nine-hole golf course.

The Big Room

The large room is the ballroom of the *Titanic*. The barman went back to get a bottle of brandy for the lifeboat, but he never made it.

The Bookmark

The man argues that he can use the dollar bill itself as a bookmark, and then spend it whenever he likes.

Bostonian

He was born in Boston, Massachusetts, in the early eighteenth century when it was still a British colony. He was British.

Brush-off

Amanda hangs up while she herself is speaking. She can subsequently claim they were disconnected.

By the River

The man was about to start a boat race by firing a starting pistol.

Call Box

She told the telephone company that people were making free international telephone calls because of a fault in the call box. They promptly sent an engineer to fix it.

Capsize

The riverboat was crowded with passengers and was motoring down a tropical river when a large snake fell off an overhanging branch onto the boat. All the passengers rushed to the other side of the boat to get away from the snake. This unbalanced the boat, which capsized.

Car in the River

The water in the river came up to the man's chest.

Catching a Bullet

The first man fires the bullet vertically. The second man is standing at the top of a cliff. The bullet just reaches the top of its flight near the top of the cliff and it falls gently into the man's outstretched hand.

The problem can be restated so that the bullet is fired horizontally, in which case the solution is as follows:

A man fires a bullet from the back of a jet plane which is flying horizontally at the exact speed of the bullet and in the opposite direction to that of the bullet. Relative to the ground the bullet has no horizontal velocity. It would fall into the hand of a man standing under the plane at the point where the bullet was fired.

The Cicada

It is believed that the 17-year life cycle gives an advantage because 17 is a prime number. Consequently, it is most unlikely that any predator would have a life cycle in synchronization with this cicada. If there were a large population of cicada one year and a consequent increase in predators, then the cicada offspring generation, which would emerge in 17 years, would not coincide with a large generation of predators because their life cycles would not be factors of 17.

The Circle and the Line

They were travelling in a hot-air balloon. When the circular circumference of the balloon crossed an electric power line, the balloon crashed and its passengers were killed.

The Circular Table

She cuts out a piece of paper exactly the size of the table. She folds the paper in half twice, along any two diameters (by easily matching opposite sides of the circle). Where the two folds meet is the center. She then places the paper on top of the table.

The Clinch

Their teeth braces were locked.

The Cloth

The man who died was shot in a duel. The man who waved

the cloth gave the signal that the two duellists could commence.

The Code

The correct answer to "Ten" is "Three." The code is the number of letters in the first word.

Confectionery Manufacturer

The workers are bees in a beehive.

The Container

A ring.

Cowardly Act

During World War I, some soldiers in the trenches deliberately exposed their hands or feet during heavy gunfire in the hope of sustaining an injury that would gain them a discharge and so avoid the risk of death.

The Crash

One of the two trucks was a car transporter carrying six brand-new cars.

Creepy Crawlies

He asks the managers of his local cinema, bars and community halls for the old cigarette ends, or butts, collected from containers. This debris they gladly give him in abundance, and he boils and strains the material to form a lethal nicotine-based insecticide which he uses to kill all the pests in his garden.

Dead Drunk

He was at a deserted underground railway station. He urinated onto the electrified third rail, making a circuit to earth, and was electrocuted.

The Deadly Diamonds

The thief simply took the box, turned it upside down, tilted it, and slid open the lid. The diamonds rolled out.

The Deadly Melody

The woman was alone and asleep in her house in the middle of the night when she was awakened by the sound of her musical jewel box. She knew that a burglar was in her bedroom. She reached under her pillow, pulled out a gun and shot him.

Depressurization

The rattle he heard was a rattlesnake that had somehow got into the plane. By depressurizing the plane, he starved the snake of oxygen and it died. He was wearing an oxygen mask and survived.

Desert

It was a very cold desert. He survived by eating snow or ice.

Doctor's Appointment

The woman explained that she was the telephone repair engineer and had come to fix the phone. The new doctor had been lying about making the calls.

Dogs Home

He could only see half of the sign on the back of the truck because one door was open and the other closed. The full sign read DOGSON'S HOME PRODUCE. It was a delicatessen's van.

Dud Car

Nova means "won't go" in Spanish.

Elevator

The woman was from out of town and had heard stories of violence and muggings in the big city. She found herself alone in an elevator with a large, fearsome-looking man who had a big Alsatian dog. The man said, "Sit, Lady!"

The terrified woman sat down only to see the dog do the same. The man cheerfully helped her up and they had a laugh about the incident.

Fair Deal

The police arrested the dealer and charged her with murder.

The Fall

He was on a roller coaster.

Fall of the Hall

The building was owned by the National Geological Society, although it had not been originally designed for them. Over the years, the society's collection of rock specimens grew and eventually the weight of the rocks caused the building to collapse.

Fall of the Wall

The guards were bribed.

40 Feet Ahead

The man walked around the Earth. Since he was walking on the surface of a sphere, his head, which was 6 feet farther away from the center of the sphere than his feet, travelled 2 pi × 6 feet farther. (It can be argued that it is impossible to walk around the Earth, but this does not matter.

Any walk of any distance on the surface of the Earth involves the same principle. A walk of 26,000 miles on the Earth's surface would mean that the man's head travelled about 40 feet farther than his feet.)

Gaze Away

The man was the King of England. Until comparatively recently, it was considered very bad manners to look directly at the monarch. People were expected to look down or away, and never in the King's face.

Good-bye, Mother

The young woman was presented with the bill for the old lady's meal. The lady had assured the waiter, "My daughter will pay."

A Hairy Story

She shaved her head!

The Hasty Packer

She was a sky diver who packed her parachute too quickly. It did not deploy correctly when she pulled the ripcord.

The Hasty Robber

He was fleeing from the scene of the crime and failed to see a police officer with a radar gun. He was stopped for speeding and ultimately convicted of robbery.

Heartless

He was a mime artist giving a stage performance. When he had the heart attack, the audience thought it was all part of the act and no one came to help him until it was too late.

The Helicopter

The helicopter was hovering just over the helicopter landing pad on an oil platform out at sea.

Holy Orders

A child had released a helium-filled balloon in the church. It was high out of reach but clearly visible. The priest was going to shoot it down with an air gun.

How to Choose a Builder

He asked each builder to nominate an alternate in case he could not take up the contract. He gave the contract to the builder most often nominated as backup.

Invaluable

The man stole a lottery ticket. It turned out to be a winning ticket for a big prize. If it had been a small prize, he could have claimed it safely and anonymously at any lottery shop. To claim a large prize he would have to report to the authorities. He did not know where the ticket had been bought. If the original owner went to the police, then it was likely the man could be identified as a thief and sent to prison. So he threw the ticket away.

Job Lot

The bricks he had bought were designed for building a chimney. They were all slightly curved and consequently of no use to the builder.

Keys in the Car

The man had already phoned his wife, who was 100 miles away, and persuaded her to drive to him with the spare set of keys. He does not want to have to explain to her that her journey was unnecessary, and face her wrath.

Kid Stuff

The expert believes that some drivers mistake children for adults and subconsciously assume that, because the figures are small, the children are farther away than they actually are.

Library Lunacy

The library was moving to new premises but had very little money for the move. By giving the borrowers extra time, it ensured that borrowers moved most of the books.

The Lifeboat

It was a wooden lifeboat. The wood swelled after two days at sea and sealed its own leaks.

The Lumberjacks

Joe uses his breaks to sharpen his axe.

The Man Who Returned Too Soon

His home was a houseboat on the sea. He put on his scuba gear and dived 200 feet. One should ascend from such a depth slowly in order to depressurize. He came up too quickly and suffered a severe attack of the "bends," from which he died.

Mickey Mouse's Girlfriend

During the Battle of the Bulge in World War II, German soldiers speaking very good English and wearing American uniforms infiltrated the American forces to confuse and misdirect them. This question was designed to identify the impostors.

The Missing Diamond

The thief had left a tape recorder in the room which had

recorded the sound of the man opening and closing the safe. From the number of clicks the thief was able to work out the combination. (He could not tell whether to go left or right initially with the dial, so he tried each option in turn.)

Murder in the Newspaper

The old man was a priest and he was sitting alone when he read the newspaper. That day a man had confessed to him that he had murdered his aunt for her money. The priest realized that the woman in the newspaper was the murder victim. The seal of the confessional meant that he could not report the incident to the police.

Mutilation

He had committed a murder. His fingerprints had been found at the scene of the crime but his identity was not yet known to the police. He dipped the ends of his fingers in acid to destroy his fingerprints.

New Shoes

She was a knife-thrower's assistant in a circus act. He was blindfolded and threw knives at her with unerring accuracy. Unfortunately her new shoes had much higher heels than her normal shoes. Therefore, she died.

The Nonchalant Police Officer

The police officer saw the incident on a TV screen in the window of a consumer electronics store. It was his favorite police-drama program!

Nun-plussed

The nun was suffering from severe hiccups. The doctor examined her and told her she was pregnant. The shock cured her hiccups, but she ran out before he could explain that his "diagnosis" was only a ruse to rid her of the hiccups.

Orange Trick

Put it under the table.

Paddle Your Own Canoe

This incident took place in Australia, where, at a certain time of year, the rains create a river that flows down a course and then eventually dries up. Effectively, the river is a body of water that moves from one point to another, then disappears.

The Painter

He had painted the walls at the art galleries.

The Painting

She said that this was the room where she meditated while standing on her head and that she had hung it upside down so she could view it as she meditated.

The Parcel

The parcel contained her husband's sandwiches, which he had forgotten to take to work. He worked in the lost property office of the bus company.

The Perfect Murder

Edward placed a tray on the edge of the kitchen table. He put some pans on one side of the tray and ice cubes on the other side. When eventually the ice melted, the weight of the pans caused the tray to fall off the table. The pans bounced on the floor and the alarm was activated. To the police, the tray, pans and water looked to be part of the general disturbance in the kitchen.

Poor Dogs

During WWII, German soldiers trained dogs to carry

explosive charges under tanks and then wait there until the charge exploded, destroying dog and tank. They then released the dogs near Russian tank positions. Unfortunately for the Germans, Russian tanks did not smell at all like the German tanks on which the dogs had been trained, so the dogs hunted around until they found German tanks to sit under. Consequently, they had to be shot and the whole sorry scheme abandoned.

Poor Impersonation

The heiress had a mannerism whereby she leaned her head to the left as she spoke. The actress rehearsed her gestures in front of a mirror, so she leaned her head to the right.

Precognition

The lady was a postal worker delivering a registered letter addressed to Mrs. Turner.

Radio Death

The man is a disc jockey who during his show put on a long piece of music and slipped out of the studio in order to kill his wife. He had timed the plan perfectly and would claim that he was on air throughout the evening as his alibi. After killing the woman, he drove hurriedly back and turned on the radio. He heard the music repeating as the record skipped. He knew that his cover was blown and he shot himself.

Rare Event

The numbers of the year 1961 read the same if you turned it upside down. This will not happen again until 6009.

Red Light

The teenagers were travelling on the road that crossed the

road the police officer was on. They drove through a green light.

Regular Arguments

They were acting in a play which involved a violent argument.

Sacrifice

One of the three was a strict vegetarian. He agreed that he should naturally be the sacrifice.

School Friend

Joe's old school friend was a woman called Louise.

Sell More Beer

The management consultant noticed that the barman was giving short measure. He told the barman to fill the glasses up to the top!

The Sign

The car was stationary. The man's wife was deaf and dumb. She used sign language to tell her husband that she was having an affair with another man and that she was leaving him.

Smart Appearance

The mortuary had prepared Victor well for his funeral.

The Sniper

He pours away the water and fills the bottle with gasoline from the car. He stuffs the handkerchief into the top of the bottle to make a Molotov cocktail. He waits until the sniper approaches the car and then lights the handkerchief before hurling the bottle at his attacker.

A Solution of Paint

Samuel Plimsoll initiated a movement which led the British in 1875, and subsequently other nations, to draw a line, the Plimsoll line, on the hull of every cargo ship showing the maximum depth to which the ship could be loaded. Prior to this, many ships had sunk because they were overloaded.

Speeding Ticket

In the very early days of motoring, the speed limit was 8 miles per hour.

Steer Clear of the Banks

The man was disabled. He got out of his car and onto his wheelchair. He used the wheelchair to go up and down the main street.

Stolen Finger

He had faked his own kidnapping and demanded a large ransom. He sent in someone else's finger with his ring on it to add force to the ransom demand.

Strange Reactions

They worked as testers in a chemical testing factory. Joan was testing an onion substitute while John was testing laughing gas.

Striking the Elephant

The man is playing billiards (or snooker or pool) with balls made of ivory. By pocketing a ball with his cue, he wins the match.

Stringing Along

The man was taking part in a kite-flying competition. He

glued tiny pieces of glass to his kite strings so that they would cut the strings of competitors' kites. He won the competition, but was subsequently disqualified.

The Suitcase and the Box

The man had just been released from prison. While there, he had caught and painstakingly trained a cockroach. It was kept in a little box and could do tricks. He went into a bar to celebrate his release and got the cockroach to do one of its tricks on the bar. He called to the bartender, "Hey, look at this." Whereupon the bartender killed it with a blow from his towel, saying, "That's the third one today!"

Sweet in Pocket

In 1945, Percy Le Baron Spencer, an engineer at Raytheon who was working on radar equipment, noticed that a candy in his pocket had melted. He correctly deduced that this was caused by microwave radiation that had agitated the molecules in the sweet. Following this discovery, Raytheon designed and patented the world's first microwave oven.

Sweet Wheat

Wheat pollinates by wind. The farmer is protecting his own future crops from contamination by inferior pollen from his neighbors' crops.

T-Shirts

A law was introduced making the wearing of seat belts compulsory for car drivers and passengers. Many Italians tried to circumvent the law. They wore the T-shirts in order to give the false impression that they were wearing seat belts.

Third Place

The man was Charlie Chaplin. While on holiday he entered a Charlie Chaplin look alike competition but he was placed third!

Thirsty

His home was his ocean-going yacht. He lost his way and his radio following a storm on an ocean voyage and eventually ran out of fresh water.

Three Notes

The woman was a traffic warden who wrote out three parking tickets. The bank robber had parked a stolen car which he intended to dump after the robbery, so he threw the ticket away. The tourist was returning to Bolivia shortly, so he threw his ticket away. The priest was sad because he would have to pay his fine.

Time of Arrival

When he came in, the boy had removed his shoes and placed them on top of the morning paper.

Title Role

She received the title role in the movie *Rebecca*. Rebecca does not appear anywhere in this movie.

The Tree and the Axe

She bought a Christmas tree. After Christmas, she put it in the garden and the next day she chopped it up.

The Truck Driver

One of the wheels of the truck had worked loose and come off a little earlier. It had continued to roll along the road.

As he stood by his truck, he was hit by the runaway wheel.

Twin Trouble

Bob and Sam were born on the night that the clocks are set back for summer time. Bob was born at 1:45 A.M. Sam was born 30 minutes later. The clocks were set back one hour at 2 A.M., so Sam's official time of birth was 1:15 A.M.

The Two Drivers

This incident took place in Saudi Arabia in 1995. It is illegal for women to drive in Saudi Arabia. One driver was a man and the other a woman. The police officer arrested the woman, who was charged and convicted.

Two Jugs

The jugs were full of frozen cubes of lemonade and milk. They stayed separate even when poured into the one large vat.

Two Suitcases

The man is on his way to check or leave the baggage for storage. Now he only has to pay for one item.

The Typist

Typing eleven words per minute is going quite fast, if the language is Chinese!

The Unlucky Gambler

The unlucky gambler had drawn a "ticket" bearing the number $6\frac{7}{8}$, i.e., the hat label with the size marked on it.

Untying the Ropes

When the President was shot he was rushed to the hospital in a serious condition. When he died, all the ropes on the flagpoles across the country were loosened, as the flags were flown at half-mast.

Well Dressed

If it was someone she wanted to invite in, she said she had just come in. If it was someone she did not want to invite in, then she said she was just about to go out.

Westward Ho!

(West) Bristol ———— Reading — —— London (East)

The two men walked to the railway station in Reading and boarded the train for Bristol at its western end. They walked to the restaurant car in the center of the train and had a long lunch. They then carried on walking east along the train, which arrived in Bristol.

WALLY Test

1. None.
2. It is best to take a photograph of a man with a camera.
3. All of them.
4. The window.
5. He drove in reverse.
6. Neither. The plane was over the Gulf of Mexico, so they both hit water.
7. Nine.
8. Most nuns use spoons.
9. To make the elevator move.
10. Lend me $13!
11. Time to get a new clock!
12. Two men, one of whom was a grandfather.
13. The archaeologist was right, of course. The coin had been found in a cloth which was carbon dated 200 B.C.
14. a) white; b) water (most people say milk).

Now rate your score on the following scale:

Number Right	Rating
12 to 14	WALLY Whiz
8 to 11	Smart Alec
4 to 7	WALLY
0 to 3	Ultra-WALLY

INDEX

Page key: **puzzle**, *clue*, solution

About the Authors

PAUL SLOANE was born in Scotland and grew up near Blackpool in the north of England. He studied engineering at Trinity Hall, Cambridge, and graduated with a first-class honors degree. While at Cambridge he met his wife, Ann, who is a teacher. They live in Camberley, England, with their three daughters.

Most of Paul Sloane's career has been in the computer industry and he is currently the European vice-president for a software company. He has always been an avid collector and creator of puzzles. His first book, *Lateral Thinking Puzzlers*, was published by Sterling in 1991. Paul Sloane has given speeches and radio talks on the topic of change management and lateral thinking.

DES MACHALE was born in County Mayo, Ireland, and is Associate Professor of Mathematics at University College in Cork. He was educated at University College, Galway, and the University of Keele in England. He and his wife, Anne, have five children.

The author of over thirty books, mostly of humor but also one on giving up smoking, Des MacHale has many interests including puzzles, geology, writing, broadcasting, films, photography, numismatics, and, of course, mathematics. He is currently working on several new projects.

This is the fourth book co-authored by Paul Sloane and Des MacHale, following on the success of their other lateral thinking puzzle books also published by Sterling.

Lateral Thinking Puzzle Books
by Paul Sloane and Des MacHale

••

Lateral Thinking Puzzlers
Paul Sloane, 1991
0-8069-8227-6

Challenging Lateral Thinking Puzzles
Paul Sloane & Des MacHale, 1993
0-8069-8671-9

Great Lateral Thinking Puzzles
Paul Sloane & Des MacHale, 1994
0-8069-0553-0

Test Your Lateral Thinking IQ
Paul Sloane, 1994
0-8069-0684-7

Improve Your Lateral Thinking:Puzzles to Challenge Your Mind
Paul Sloane & Des MacHale, 1995
0-8069-1374-6

Intriguing Lateral Thinking Puzzles
Paul Sloane & Des MacHale, 1996
0-8069-4252-5

••

Ask for them wherever books are sold.